To: The Soaring Eagle Basketball Team

May God give you a new life so you may run and not be weary and walk and not be faint.

God bless,
Eric R. Jackson 3/2016

A NEW LIFE
THE ONLY WAY TO WIN

ERIC RONALD JACKSON

WESTBOW
PRESS®
A DIVISION OF THOMAS NELSON
& ZONDERVAN

Scripture taken from the New King James Version. Copyright © 1979, 1980,
1982 by Thomas Nelson, Inc. Used by permission. All rights reserved.

Scripture taken from the King James Version of the Bible.

Scripture taken from the Holy Bible, NEW INTERNATIONAL VERSION®.
Copyright © 1973, 1978, 1984 by Biblica, Inc. All rights reserved worldwide.
Used by permission. NEW INTERNATIONAL VERSION® and NIV® are registered
trademarks of Biblica, Inc. Use of either trademark for the offering of goods
or services requires the prior written consent of Biblica US, Inc.

WestBow Press books may be ordered through booksellers or by contacting:

WestBow Press
A Division of Thomas Nelson & Zondervan
1663 Liberty Drive
Bloomington, IN 47403
www.westbowpress.com
1 (866) 928-1240

Because of the dynamic nature of the Internet, any web addresses or
links contained in this book may have changed since publication and
may no longer be valid. The views expressed in this work are solely those
of the author and do not necessarily reflect the views of the publisher,
and the publisher hereby disclaims any responsibility for them.

Any people depicted in stock imagery provided by Thinkstock are models,
and such images are being used for illustrative purposes only.
Certain stock imagery © Thinkstock.

ISBN: 978-1-5127-2737-1 (sc)
ISBN: 978-1-5127-2738-8 (hc)
ISBN: 978-1-5127-2736-4 (e)

Library of Congress Control Number: 2016900864

Print information available on the last page.

WestBow Press rev. date: 02/08/2016

Contents

Foreword

Those who claim to have salvation usually respond to the questions "Are you saved?" or "Are you a Christian?" with various answers. Many times the answers do not reflect a true knowledge of the "new birth" as specified in the Scriptures. Oftentimes misconceptions result from answers that are based on traditions or beliefs but not on sound biblical truth.

In his discussion of the "new birth," Brother Eric Jackson explores both the physical and spiritual processes involved with salvation. His work is stimulating and goes right to the "embryo" of the true spiritual birth. His emphasis on the life processes is challenging and presents a deep, spiritual reality in a very understandable way. Furthermore, Brother Jackson offers biblically based, practical and spiritual truths, which every believer would be wise to use as a divining rod of his or her new birth experience.

A New Life: The Only Way to Win offers readers exactly that—a new life—and is a welcomed and much-needed book for the church, especially for individuals seeking reality in salvation. Life involves both a physical and a spiritual journey. Therefore, you need good directions to reach your desired destination. This book can serve as a dependable road map on your journey to a "new life." I pray God will bless your life as you read it and engraft its message in your heart.

Reverend Carl E. Jenkins, Sr., EdM,
Former pastor of Dale City Christian Church (Dale City, Virginia)

Preface

I am publishing this book again to make it available to those who did not get a copy of the first printing. Other than editorial changes, this edition is basically the same as the first edition.

Prior to the undertaking of the first edition, I had not given much thought to writing a book. However, a series of events occurred that brought me great joy and motivated me to write.

Several years before the first edition, Mr. Donald Charity, a fellow Sunday school teacher, and I were explaining the process of becoming a Christian to a newly organized class for single adults. After the class discussed this subject, I continued to study the process. As I studied, the Holy Spirit showed me how similar the spiritual birth is to the physical birth. The more I studied, the more I appreciated the wonderful knowledge I gained. This knowledge made me want to share this exciting information with others. That's when the idea of writing a booklet came to me. At first I thought it would be a booklet because I was thinking of only publishing the analogy of the two births. However, the Lord had more for me to write.

Although the first chapter compares the physical and the spiritual births, the primary focus of the book is to provide information to help people build a strong spiritual foundation for their "new lives" in Jesus Christ. This foundation will "let us run with patience the race that is set before us" (Hebrews 12:1 KJV). As you read this book, I pray that the Holy Spirit will reveal to you the same joy, knowledge, conviction, and appreciation of God's Word as He gave me while studying and writing it.

Thanks to Dr. Becky Stephenson for reviewing the physical birth process sections of chapter 1.

I would like to give my appreciation to the Standard Publishing Company for the use of the information I collected from their Sunday school lessons, Zondervan Publishing House for allowing me to use quotations from the New International Version of the Bible, and Hendrickson Publishers for allowing me to paraphrase excerpts from *Matthew Henry's Commentary on the Whole Bible*.

Eric Ronald Jackson

Acknowledgments

Many people and resources helped me acquire the information for this book and publish its first edition. First of all, I thank the Father, Son, and Holy Spirit for the inspiration, insight, and wisdom to write this book.

I want to thank Rev. Carl E. Jenkins, former pastor of the Dale City Christian Church, for the spiritual review and advice that improved the manuscript. He found time in his busy schedule to perform a thorough review of the first draft and later discussed his comments with me.

I also thank my family for their support. A special thank-you goes to my wife, Celestine, who constantly tolerated my disappearances to a room to prepare and correct the manuscript. She encouraged me throughout the book preparation process.

I thank Donald Charity, my former, fellow Sunday school teacher, for engaging in stimulating discussions on spiritual topics and for reviewing the manuscript for the first edition.

CHAPTER 1

Comparison of Physical and Spiritual Births

Very truly I tell you, no one can see the kingdom of God unless they are born again ... Flesh gives birth to flesh, but the Spirit gives birth to spirit (John 3:3, 6 NIV).

These powerful words Jesus shared with Nicodemus, a Jewish religious leader who came to Him at night inquiring about salvation, show us that there are two births—one physical and one spiritual. The apostle Paul also says in 1 Corinthians 15:44, "It [the body] is sown a natural body, it is raised a spiritual body. There is a natural body, and there is a spiritual body" (NKJV). The Holy Spirit revealed to me that even though the births are different, they are remarkably similar. The spiritual birth is the most important because

1

it is required for anyone who wants to enter the kingdom of God.

To see the similarities between the two births, we must consider seven events of the physical life. Within each event, some factors of the physical life are identified and the corresponding factors of the spiritual life are given. Throughout the comparisons, remember that spiritual birth events are not restricted by time as physical birth events are. We will use seven physical life events for this discussion:

1. Conception
2. Development
3. Premature Birth
4. Full-Term Birth
5. Time of Birth
6. Infancy
7. Growth

1. Conception

Physical Birth

The physical birth process begins when a female's ovary releases an egg. The egg travels from the ovary through the fallopian tube to the uterus. If the egg is fertilized by a male's sperm, it attaches itself to the lining of the uterus and starts to develop. If the egg is not fertilized by a sperm, it dies and is discarded. To fertilize an egg, a sperm must penetrate the outer covering of the egg and unite with it. The fertilized egg is the beginning of a new human life.

Spiritual Birth

In this comparison, the spiritual life process begins when a person is born physically. The physical "egg" can be compared to the undeveloped, spiritual heart, which resides in the body. However, unlike the egg, the spiritual heart does not travel. The "uterus" can be compared to the human body, which holds the spiritual heart. The "lining of the uterus" can be compared to the subconscious or decision-making part of the body. Similarly, the "sperm" can be compared to the Word of God.

From this viewpoint, a spark of spiritual life begins when a person's spiritual heart receives the true Word of God and not a fabrication of His Word. To unite a person with the Word of God, the person's "outer covering" made of such things as ignorance, prejudices, bad experiences, doubt, etc., must be penetrated. When a heart is capable of receiving God's Word, it is humble, broken, willing to learn from its mistakes, ready to change, searching for happiness, and longing for peace. If a person's spiritual heart is never exposed to God's Word, it is not fertilized and the new birth as described herein does not apply to it: "So then faith cometh by hearing, and hearing by the word of God" (Romans 10:17 KJV).

2. Development

Physical Birth

During fertilization, chromosomes from the egg and the sperm pass on many of the parents' characteristics to the embryo. After the egg is fertilized, it attaches itself to the lining of the uterus, and the female becomes pregnant. For the first two to eight weeks after fertilization, this union of egg and sperm is called an embryo. During the second week of embryo development, a structure called the placenta forms. The placenta consists of tissues and blood vessels that surround the embryo and connect it to the uterus. The umbilical cord connects the placenta to the embryo and serves as the "lifeline" that carries food, water, and oxygen from the mother to the developing child. The umbilical cord also carries waste material from the embryo back to the mother.

When the mother eats nutritious and healthy food, drinks proper liquids, and breathes air that does not contain harmful levels of pollution, the embryo grows properly— unless a medical condition exists that prevents proper growth. However, if the mother eats unwholesome food, consumes harmful drugs and liquids, or breathes heavily polluted air, the embryo could become distorted or possibly die (a miscarriage).

Spiritual Birth

After the spiritual heart is impregnated with God's Word, it develops similarly to the embryo. The spiritual heart develops according to the person's background and environment and to God's direction.

Unlike the embryo, who receives food from one person, the spiritual heart receives its "food" (information) from one or more of a person's senses, such as sight and hearing. The mind carries the information from the senses to the spiritual heart. This makes it comparable to the umbilical cord. Just as what the mother eats affects the growth of the embryo, the spiritual heart is either nourished or deprived by what it is fed by the mind. Therefore, to ensure a healthy, spiritual development, a person must continually hear the unadulterated Word of God and be influenced by the guidance and lives of mature Christians. Hearing the Word and receiving godly influence also help the mind remove "waste" (old habits, beliefs, etc.).

Like the physical embryo who receives unwholesome food, a person who receives distorted information about God, Jesus, and the Holy Spirit could suffer adverse effects. Receiving distorted information and untruths about the Trinity (Father, Son, and Holy Spirit) results in confusion and misconceptions. This might make it harder for the person to understand the truth and grow spiritually, or worse, the person might become so frustrated that he gives up completely and dies spiritually, which compares to a physical miscarriage.

3. Premature Birth

Physical Birth

A premature physical birth occurs when a baby is born before the thirty-seventh week after conception. (A full-term pregnancy is approximately forty weeks.) Although no one knows exactly what causes a baby to be born prematurely, there are some likely causes:

1. The woman may have been a premature baby herself or may have had a premature baby before.
2. During pregnancy, the woman may have received inadequate medical care or nutrition.
3. The woman may have been under the age of sixteen or over the age of forty.
4. Lifestyles involving stressful careers, occupations requiring strenuous physical effort, and smoking may have increased the risk of premature labor.

A premature baby's survival depends on his degree of development and health at birth. Survival also depends on the availability of lifesaving equipment. However, the tender loving care given by parents and caregivers is very important.

A premature birth can cause the parents to experience some of the most painful emotions of their lives. Deep feelings of guilt, anxiety, or grief are likely. Additionally, parents are faced with extra work and expenses during the child's first months. Therefore, expectant mothers and fathers should take every possible precaution to decrease the risk of a premature birth.

Spiritual Birth

Premature spiritual birth occurs when a person thinks he is saved before he has had a true change of heart. The following examples explain how this devastating result can occur:

1. A person may compare himself with other premature Christians.
2. Someone other than a spiritually led and mature Christian may tell the person who wants to be saved that he is saved based on his actions alone.

3. A person may be coerced into making a public confession of his new spiritual birth before he is ready.

4. A person may not fully understand what is required by the Word of God to be born spiritually.

A person's survival after a premature spiritual birth depends on his degree of spiritual development at "birth." Spiritual survival also depends on the availability of "lifesaving" techniques, such as intercessory prayer and the important tender loving care given by Christians.

When someone intimidates, embarrasses, or does anything to cause someone else to make an "instant" decision about salvation, he may be setting the foundation for a premature spiritual birth. In Matthew 28:19–20, Jesus told Christians to go and teach all nations to obey everything He commanded. (Note that Jesus said to *teach* all nations to obey everything He commanded.) Some good intentions can have damaging effects. Christian leaders and laymen should exercise special care to avoid pushing a person to verbally accept Christ before he has actually experienced regeneration.

However, there are many positive ways Christians can encourage others to accept Jesus Christ as their Lord and Savior and thereby allow them to experience the new birth. One way is to tell people the requirements and benefits of salvation. This will help people understand the value and cost of having a relationship with God through acceptance of His Son, Jesus Christ. Also, Christians can humbly share their testimonies of becoming born again, "saved," and thereby let people know the new birth is possible.

Spiritual leaders should examine their motives and procedures for inviting people to accept Christ as their personal Savior and Lord. They should make sure they are not setting the stage for Satan* to influence or pressure a person to outwardly accept Jesus Christ before he inwardly (within his heart) accepts Him. For example, when people are invited to accept Christ, the spiritual leader should not ask the people of the congregation to close their eyes just to encourage someone to come forward and proclaim his acceptance of Christ. However, the leader could ask the people of the congregation to bow their heads, to close their eyes, and to pray for those who need to accept Christ or learn about Him and His plan of salvation.

*Satan, also called the Devil, is the Christian's enemy. He is the ruler of this world who seeks to alienate mankind from God by deceiving and destroying them. (See John 12:31, 1 Peter 5:8, and Revelation 12:9.)

4. Full-Term Birth

Physical Birth

After approximately five weeks, the embryo takes on a shape that represents the characteristics of his parents. After the ninth week, the growing organism, or fetus, looks much like a human baby. The time before birth is important and exciting. In addition to the increased size of the expectant mother's midsection, the mother is assured of the life inside her by the occasional kicks or movement of the fetus, which usually occurs after the fourth month. A new life is about to be introduced into a new world. Although this is an exciting and anxious time for the mother, she should not do things that could lead to an early labor. She should be patient and allow God to be in control.

Spiritual Birth

As a person's spiritual heart continues to grow by hearing and studying the Word of God, much like the "fetus," his spiritual life begins to take shape. Some of his actions and thoughts reflect those of a Christian's. This phase in one's spiritual life is also exciting and important. The Christian "caregivers" of this developing spiritual person look forward to the birth of this new life. However, in all the excitement, "mothering" Christians should be content with planting and watering the seed and let God give the increase. (See 1 Corinthians 3:5–9.)

A person's spiritual birth must come from within. He must hear and receive the Word of God so that he is convinced Jesus is Lord and Savior of his life. (Chapter 2 elaborates on this point further.)

5. Time of Birth

Physical Birth

Approximately nine months after the sperm fertilizes the egg, birth occurs. At that time, the baby is delivered from the mother's womb and the physician or midwife ties and cuts the umbilical cord. He leaves the womb (his previous "home") and begins a new life (his new "home"). However, he is helpless, fragile, and completely dependent on others for survival. For several months, he can't even support his own head.

Spiritual Birth

A person is spiritually born when he confesses with his mouth that Jesus is Lord and believes in his heart that God raised Jesus from the dead. (Refer to Romans 10:9.)

Sometimes the exact "time" of a person's true spiritual birth may not be apparent to that individual. (See Chapter 2 of this book.) At the time of his confession, he may believe with his mind that God raised Jesus from the dead and that Jesus is his Lord and Savior, but may not believe with his heart until later.

A spiritual birth is not always as spontaneous or emotional as a physical birth. A spiritual birth requires that a person has an abiding conviction to no longer follow the ways of the world but to follow the ways of God, as revealed in His Word. When a person receives this conviction, he willingly prays the sinner's prayer. In this prayer, he acknowledges that he is a sinner, accepts Jesus as his personal Savior and Lord, and asks Jesus to come into his life and to forgive him of all his sins. The new birth becomes a reality. The requirement for salvation that Jesus explained to Nicodemus is fulfilled. (See John 3:3–7.)

When the new birth occurs, the new Christian is not separated, like the physical birth, from his nurturing source, as the severing of the umbilical cord. His lifeline gets connected to a greater source than before—heaven. Although physical babies are not totally covered with blood, the new Christian is "covered" with blood, for he has been washed with the blood of Jesus. He has a new life in an old home, which is his body. Therefore, he must prepare himself for his new home, which is heaven. However, unlike a physical newborn, who is helpless at physical birth, the new Christian must learn to be "helpless" and completely dependent on God. When he is not dependent on the Godhead (Father, Son, and Holy Spirit), he may find he cannot use his "head" to make wise choices. Because he is fragile, he is likely to be an easy target for Satan's deceptions and temptations.

6. Infancy

Physical Life

A child born to loving parents receives love, food, and necessities for life. For the first few months, his food is limited to his mother's milk or a milk substitute.

Infancy is an important event in a child's formative years. Therefore in addition to food, the baby's environment is also important. Some children share quality time with their parents while worshipping God, eating meals together, doing chores together, and doing other things together. Children who spend quality time with their families seem to have higher self-esteem than children who spend little time in a family environment. They also seem to be less inclined to consume illegal drugs or to smoke tobacco products.

Spiritual Life

Many new Christians are often referred to as "baby" or "carnal" Christians because their actions, at times, may not be much different from their old lifestyles. (See Chapter 2.) Carnal Christians can only receive the milk of the Word. (The milk of the Word refers those basic Scriptures that are easily understood by new Christians.) Their lifestyles may be characterized by selfishness, greed, quarreling, jealousy, pride, and other worldly desires they had before conversion.

For some Christians, this stage of development can be frustrating because they become prime targets for Satan's attacks. Since baby Christians' knowledge of God's Word—which is their food—may be limited, the devil can deceive new Christians to doubt their salvation or mislead them to believe false doctrines.

Quality "family" time for the new Christian is as important as it is for the physical infant. New Christians can deal with life's problems and Satan's temptations more effectively when they have spiritual families who are willing to spend quality time with them. Therefore, in addition to putting forth tremendous efforts to bring souls to Christ, churches should put forth similar efforts to help new converts grow in the knowledge of our Lord and Savior, Jesus Christ.

God, our heavenly Father, depends on the church to be His caregiver for new Christians. Therefore the church should provide opportunities for new Christians to grow spiritually or at least tell Christians where to find those opportunities. Likewise, new Christians should take advantage of as many opportunities as they can wisely schedule.

7. Growth

Physical Life

Mental growth and physical growth are greatly influenced by what a person allows to enter his mind and body. The greatest influence seems to be love. A child who receives love becomes inspired to face the challenges of life. Although the child falls when attempting his first steps, the presence of a loving parent makes it easier for that child to get up and try again. Parents know walking requires taking one step at a time. However, no matter how much the parents want a child to walk, the child is the one who decides when to take the first steps.

As the child grows, his food changes from liquids to a mixture of liquids and solids. The parents introduce the solids gradually. They start with a finely strained mixture and slowly increase the size of the particles until the child can handle larger pieces of food. The size of food the child can safely consume depends on the maturity of that child. Loving parents introduce solids into their child's diet because they don't want him to remain an infant forever.

They want their child to mature to an adult stage. Therefore, they train the child to eat the foods adults eat, provided there is no medical problem to hinder them.

Spiritual Life

Spiritual growing from a carnal to a mature Christian is greatly influenced by what a person allows to come into his mind, heart, and body. Just as in the physical life, the greatest influence seems to be love. Christians who receive love are inspired to face life's challenges. Although new Christians make mistakes while taking their first steps as spiritual babes, the presence of loving, mature Christians makes it easier for them to use their mistakes to improve their Christian walks. Like a young child, a new Christian has to take one step at a time. Therefore, no matter how much older Christians want new Christians to change their lifestyles, new Christians are the ones who decide when to take their first steps.

Like a child, the new Christian's food should gradually change as he grows spiritually. Hebrews 5:12–14 says, "You need milk, not solid food! Anyone who lives on milk, being still an infant, is not acquainted with the teaching about righteousness. But solid food is for the mature, who by constant use have trained themselves to distinguish good from evil" (NIV). Christians reach spiritual maturity when they develop and practice discernment and sound judgment.

The following table gives a condensed comparison of the physical and spiritual lives:

Physical Birth	Spiritual Birth
female's egg	undeveloped spiritual heart
uterus	human body
lining of uterus	subconscious or decision-making part of the body
male's sperm	Word of God
embryo	spiritual heart becomes alive
umbilical cord	mind
nourished by wholesome food	nourished by the unadulterated Word of God
premature baby's survival depends on degree of maturity and health	premature Christian's survival depends on spiritual maturity of person when he thinks he is born again
development of embryo takes time	development of spiritual heart takes time
Birth occurs after approximately nine months.	Birth occurs at the complete change of the heart.
completely dependent on others	must be completely dependent on God
food limited to milk	food is the milk of the Word
baby's environment is important	new Christian's environment is important
mental and physical growth influenced by what mind and body receives	mental and physical growth influenced by what mind, heart, and body receives

Although the analogy above represents one way of comparing the physical and spiritual births, other analogies could be developed in a similar manner. However, no matter which analogy a person uses, somewhere in the spiritual process there must be a second birth—a spiritual birth. The important point to remember about becoming a Christian is the statement Jesus proclaimed to Nicodemus in John 3:7, "You should not be surprised at my saying, 'You must be born again'" (NIV).

CHAPTER 2

Becoming a Christian

As presented in Chapter 1, Event 4: Full Term Birth, a person must keep hearing about God, Jesus, and the Holy Spirit until he is convinced that he wants Jesus as his Lord and Savior or in other words, he wants to be saved. Generally, Christians agree that the basic steps to become saved are as easy as "A, B, C:"

A. *Acknowledge, agree, or admit* you are a lost sinner and that Christ is the only one who can save you. "For all have sinned, and come short of the glory of God" (Romans 3:23 KJV).

B. *Believe* that Jesus Christ died for your sins and that He is the only one who can save you. "For God so loved the world, that he gave his only begotten Son, that whosoever believeth in him should not perish, but have everlasting life" (John 3:16 KJV).

C. *Confess* before others that Jesus Christ is your Savior and commit to following Christ. Romans 10:9 states, "That if thou shalt confess with thy mouth the Lord Jesus, and shalt believe in thine heart that God hath raised him from the dead, thou shalt be saved" (KJV). The apostle Peter also admonished people to, "Repent, and be baptized every one of you in the name of Jesus Christ for the remission of sins, and ye shall receive the gift of the Holy Ghost" (Acts 2:38 KJV).

This conversion from sinner to Christian is the beginning of a race or journey that lasts a lifetime. As our commitment grows, so does our joy until we receive our ultimate joy in heaven—to be with our Lord and Savior.

These three basic steps to salvation seem so simple some people may take them too lightly. However, each step is important because it requires a deep inward decision. Consider the key word of Step B, *believe*, and again refer to Romans 10:9, which says, "... believe in thine heart ..." In Romans 10:8 the apostle Paul says, "...The word is nigh thee, even in thy mouth, and in thy heart: that is, the word of faith, which we preach" (KJV). In Romans 10:10 he adds, "For with the heart man believeth unto righteousness; and with the mouth confession is made unto salvation" (KJV).

So we see that a person's belief must come from his heart and is based on his faith. This inward change of mind, loyalties, convictions, and motivations must occur before someone can fear God and feel sorry for sinning against Him. This change will result in outward actions that show a repentant lifestyle.

A person may ask, "How do I get this faith or this change of heart?" Paul asked a series of similar questions in Romans, "How, then, can they call on the one they have not believed in? And how can they believe in the one of whom they have not heard? And how can they hear without someone preaching to them? And how can anyone preach unless they are sent?" (10:14–15 NIV).

His answer is given in Romans 10:17, "Consequently, faith comes from hearing the message, and the message is heard through the word about Christ" (NIV). Therefore, becoming a Christian is an act of the will. This act is developed through a conviction that comes from reading the Word of God and the ministry of the Holy Spirit.

The apostle James states the following points about faith and deeds:

1. "You believe that there is one God. Good! Even the demons believe that—and shudder" (James 2:19 NIV).

2. "You see that his [Abraham] faith and his actions were working together, and *his faith was made complete by what he did*" (James 2:22 NIV, emphasis mine).

3. "You see that a person is considered righteous by what they do and not by faith alone" (James 2:24 NIV).

Note: James says that even demons believe Jesus is Lord. However, they don't practice this belief.

An excellent illustration to demonstrate the difference between belief and faith follow[1]

> A number of years ago a tight-wire artist was demonstrating his skill on a wire stretched above Niagara Falls. A large crowd watched in amazement as he made numerous trips across the wire—forward, backward. Then he asked the crowds if they believed he could walk across the wire pushing a wheelbarrow.
>
> "Yes," they exclaimed, "you can do it!"
>
> So he took a wheelbarrow and crossed back and forth on the wire again. When he returned, he asked the crowds if they believed he could walk across the wire pushing a wheelbarrow with a man riding in it.
>
> "Yes," they exclaimed, "you can do it!"

So he asked for a volunteer to assist him in this daring feat. However, the crowd became quiet as they looked at each other. No one would come forward to volunteer.

From this illustration, we see that action is the primary difference between belief and faith. Faith produces action. Therefore the decision to follow Jesus must come from the heart and must result in corresponding actions. When anyone makes this decision, his life begins to change in the way the apostle Paul describes in 2 Corinthians 5:17, "Therefore if any man be in Christ, he is a new creature: old things are passed away; behold, all things are become new" (KJV). Old habits, attitudes, priorities, etc., begin to change and to reflect the new spiritual life. For example, the person he considers *number one* in his life is replaced by Jesus.

Not only should old habits, attitudes, priorities, etc. change but they also should be forgotten. Paul says in Philippians 3:13–14, "Brethren, I count not myself to have apprehended: but this one thing I do, forgetting those things which are behind, and reaching forth unto those things which are before, I press toward the mark for the prize of the high calling of God in Christ Jesus" (KJV).

Anyone who has tried to go straight to a designated point realizes he will get off course if he takes his eyes off the destination. Therefore, focusing on Jesus and heaven rather than on past sins should be a primary goal for Christians. Past sins will then become a measuring stick for Christians to appreciate repentance.

For some Christians, the change from their old lifestyles to their new ones is dramatic and quick, but for others, it is a slow, gradual process.

The changes are similar to the ones that occur in the maple and oak trees near my house. During the fall of the year all the leaves of the maple tree will drop to the ground within a few days, whereas some of the leaves on the oak tree seem as if they are going to stay on the tree until next spring. However, as long as the oak tree remains alive, the leaves must fall before new leaves develop in the spring.

Likewise, as long as the heart is open to receive God's Word, a change will take place. Eventually, sincere Christians will find themselves growing to the point where they can share in the apostle Paul's confession in Romans 8:38–39, which says, "For I am persuaded, that neither death, nor life, nor angels, nor principalities, nor powers, nor things present, nor things to come, nor height, nor depth, nor any other creature, shall be able to separate us from the love of God, which is in Christ Jesus our Lord" (KJV).

As mentioned in Chapter 1, Event 6: Infancy, when some people become saved (born again), they are considered carnal Christians and mere infants in Christ. They are saved but do not yet live Christian lives. The apostle Paul discussed this stage of Christianity in 1 Corinthians 3:1-3, when he says, "And I, brethren, could not speak to you as to spiritual people but as to carnal, as to babes in Christ. I fed you with milk and not with solid food; for until now you were not able to receive it, and even now you are still not able; for you are still carnal. For where there are envy, strife, and divisions among you, are you not carnal and behaving like mere men?" (NKJV).

Just as physical babies must learn many things so they will grow physically and mentally, carnal Christians must also learn how to crucify ungodly and fleshly desires. In Galatians 5:16-17, Paul advises, "So I say, walk by the Spirit, and you will not gratify the desires of the flesh. For the flesh desires what is contrary to the Spirit, and the Spirit what is contrary to the flesh. They are in conflict with each other, so that you are not to do whatever you want" (NIV).

Many Christians experience this struggle. However, it can be very frustrating for carnal Christians who may ask themselves, "Why is it so hard to live a Christian life? Why do I want to do those things I did before I became a Christian? Why am I having all these problems?"

When these and similar questions arise, it's important to realize that even mature Christians can be like the apostle Paul, who could not understand why he did things that he didn't want to do. In Romans 7:14-25, he debated this dilemma within himself. He said, "I find then a law, that, when I would do good, evil is present with me" (Romans 7:21 KJV). He even considered himself to be a wretched man. Nevertheless he concludes, as should all Christians in similar situations, that God, through Jesus Christ our Lord, is the only one who can rescue him from the corruption of nature.

The apostle Paul continues his discussion of sinful nature and the Spirit in Romans 8. He tells us that if the Spirit lives in us, we are not controlled by sinful nature. People controlled by the sinful nature will want to please its desires. However, those controlled by the Spirit will want to please the desires of the Spirit. (See Romans 8:1–17.)

One way of understanding the relationships between the body, sinful nature, and the Holy Spirit is to imagine that your body has two "people" inside. One person lives only on what is good, and one lives only on what is evil. Both persons desire control of your body, mind, will, and emotions. The "person" who receives the largest amount of "food" will grow to control the actions and thoughts of your body. For example, suppose you read pornographic materials, listen to sensual music, or watch television shows that degrade the family and distort the truth. You would be feeding the "person" who lives on what is evil (the sinful nature), thereby satisfying its desires. This would cause your body to be controlled by the evil "person" within, which would prevent you from pleasing God.

Instead of doing those things, suppose you read and study the Holy Bible, listen to music that praises God and reminds you of His goodness, and watch television shows that show you the beauty of God's creation and that have educational value. You would be feeding the good "person." Then your body would be controlled by the "person" who lives on what is good (the Holy Spirit). Then the good "person" within wins control of your body, thereby pleasing God. With the Holy Spirit in control, you will develop Christian characteristics.

CHAPTER 3

Christian Characteristics

After surrendering his heart and mind to Christ, a person's life changes because his heart directs his actions to match his faith. The reality of salvation is shown through his actions. In 1 John, the apostle John gives the characteristics of a Christian.

Christian Characteristics

A Christian keeps Jesus' commandments (the Word).

> Now by this we know that we know Him, if we keep His commandments. He who says, 'I know Him,' and does not keep His commandments, is a liar, and the truth is not in him. But whoever keeps His word, truly the love of God is perfected in him. (1 John 2:3–5 NKJV)

A Christian patterns his lifestyle after Christ's.

> By this we know that we are in Him. He who says
> he abides in Him ought himself also to walk just
> as He walked. (1 John 2:5–6 NKJV)

If we want to walk like Jesus did, we should ask ourselves
the question, "What would Jesus do if He were in the same
situation I am in?"

A Christian loves other Christians as brothers.

> He who says he is in the light, and hates his brother,
> is in darkness until now ... But he who hates his
> brother is in darkness and walks in darkness, and
> does not know where he is going, because the
> darkness has blinded his eyes ... We know that we
> have passed from death to life, because we love the
> brethren. He who does not love *his* brother abides
> in death ... If someone says, 'I love God,' and hates
> his brother, he is a liar; for he who does not love
> his brother whom he has seen, how can he love
> God whom he has not seen? (1 John 2:9, 11; 3:14;
> 4:20 NKJV)

A Christian does not love the world.

> Love not the world, neither the things that are in the
> world. If any man love the world, the love of the Father
> is not in him. For all that is in the world, the lust of the
> flesh, and the lust of the eyes, and the pride of life, is
> not of the Father, but is of the world. And the world
> passeth away, and the lust thereof: but he that doeth
> the will of God abideth for ever. (1 John 2:15–17 KJV)

A Christian is anointed by the Holy Spirit.

> But you have an anointing from the Holy One, and
> you know all things. (1 John 2:20 NKJV)

The word *anointing*, when used here, does not refer to the
anointing of the body with oil but to the gift of the Holy Spirit
that allows us to have spiritual power and understanding
of the truth. Although a formal education can help us
understand certain aspects of the Bible, the mysteries of the
Bible can only come through revelations from the Holy Spirit.

A Christian remembers Jesus' teachings.

> Therefore let that abide in you which you heard
> from the beginning. If what you heard from the

beginning abides in you, you also will abide in the
Son and in the Father. (1 John 2:24 NKJV)

When Jesus resisted Satan's temptations, He quoted
Scriptures. (See Matthew 4:1–11.) One of the greatest ways
we can resist Satan is to remember what Jesus did and what
the Bible says. However, Satan doesn't wait until we have a
Bible in our hands to tempt us. So we must remember biblical
teachings and be ready to apply them so we can overcome
Satan's temptations, praise God, help others understand God,
and remain in the Son and in the Father. However, before we
can quote Scripture from memory, we must first memorize it.

A Christian does what is right.

If you know that He [God] is righteous, you know
that everyone who practices righteousness is born
of Him [God]. (1 John 2:29 NKJV)

Jesus says in Matthew 7:18, "A good tree cannot bring
forth evil fruit, neither can a corrupt tree bring forth good
fruit" (KJV). A tree is known by the fruit it bears. If you
know a tree produces apples, you call it an apple tree. You
don't look for lemons, pears, or other fruit on that tree.
Likewise, everyone born of Christ practices righteousness
because he knows that his "tree," (God) is righteous.

A Christian purifies himself.

> Beloved, now we are children of God; and it has not yet been revealed what we shall be, but we know that when He is revealed, we shall be like Him, for we shall see Him as He is. And everyone who has this hope in Him purifies himself, just as He is pure. (1 John 3:2–3 NKJV)

We purify ourselves by asking for forgiveness and repenting of our sins. We can only have this hope if we are born again and have a new spiritual life.

A Christian stops sinning.

> No one who lives in him keeps on sinning. No one who continues to sin has either seen him or known him. (1 John 3:6 NIV)

A believer's life is characterized not by sin but by doing what is right. The key words in this verse are *keeps on* and *continues.* If we continue to sin in a particular way, have we truly repented of that sin? Have we had a thorough change in our hearts toward that sin? If we know Christ, we know He alone has the power to help us overcome that sin.

John says in 1 John 1:8–10, "If we say that we have no sin, we deceive ourselves, and the truth is not in us. If we confess our sins, He is faithful and just to forgive us *our* sins and to cleanse us from all unrighteousness. If we say that we have not sinned, we make Him a liar, and His word is not in us" (NKJV). Although Jesus will forgive our sins, we should not allow it lessen our desire to stop sinning. In Romans 6:1–2, the apostle Paul wrote, "What shall we say then? Shall we continue in sin that grace may abound? Certainly not! How shall we who died to sin live any longer in it?" (NKJV).

A Christian loves with actions and in truth.

> Dear children, let us not love with words or speech but with actions and in truth. (1 John 3:18 NIV)

I love you are three wonderful words we can say to a loved one. But if they are not said in truth and are not supported by actions, they become vain and empty. Jesus requires us to love with our actions. Two examples are found in the Gospel of John.

> If ye love me, keep my commandments. (John 14:15 KJV)

> Simon, son of Jonas, lovest thou me? ... Feed my sheep. (John 21:16–17 KJV)

A Christian belongs to the truth and sets his heart at rest.

> This is how we know that we belong to the truth and how we set our hearts at rest in his presence: If our hearts condemn us, we know that God is greater than our hearts, and he knows everything. (1 John 3:19–20 NIV)

The eighteenth verse says we should love with actions and in the truth. When our faith in God grows, we trust Him, we depend more on Him, and we know He is the truth. As we grow closer to God, we know we belong to Him (the truth). Since God knows our hearts and everything about us, He knows our motives for saying and doing things. He knows when we love with actions and truth. Therefore when we are close to God, we will be in His presence. This closeness will cause our hearts to condemn us when we think about doing wrong, or do wrong, and will set our hearts at rest.

A Christian prays and receives answers.

> Dear friends, if our hearts do not condemn us, we have confidence before God and receive from him anything we ask, because we obey his commands and do what pleases him. (1 John 3:21–22 NIV)

Being obedient to God and doing what pleases Him enable us to receive anything we ask from Him. However, when we obey and please God, we should not ask for things that displease Him or are outside of His will. We must also understand that "no" is an answer and that there are some things that would benefit us more if we would wait to receive them.

A Christian tests the spirits.

> Dear friends, do not believe every spirit, but test the spirits to see whether they are from God, because many false prophets have gone out into the world. ... You, dear children, are from God and have overcome them, because the one who is in you is greater than the one who is in the world. ... We are from God, and whoever knows God listens to us; but whoever is not from God does not listen to us. This is how we recognize the Spirit of truth and the spirit of falsehood. (1 John 4:1, 4, 6 NIV)

We should not believe every person who says he is a Christian and a follower of God. We should watch to see if that person's actions support what he says. If he gives us spiritual advice, we should study the Bible and talk with spiritual leaders to see if his advice agrees with God's view on the subject. These checks will allow us to recognize the spirit of truth or the spirit of falsehood in his advice.

A Christian lives in God, and God lives in him.

> Whoever confesses that Jesus is the Son of God, God abides in him, and he in God. (1 John 4:15 NKJV)

Anyone who confesses from his heart that Jesus is the Lord and Savior of his life is saved. The Holy Spirit abides in and enriches him. Jesus says in John 15:4, "Abide in me, and I in you. As the branch cannot bear fruit of itself, except it abide in the vine; no more can ye, except ye abide in me" (KJV).

A Christian lives in love.

> And we have known and believed the love that God has for us. God is love, and he who abides in love abides in God, and God in him. (1 John 4:16 NKJV)

In the English language, our use of the word *love* is so general we need to know the context in which it is being used to understand how it is being used. Sometimes we refer to four Greek words to distinguish the types of love. The word *eros* means selfish love based on sexual desires or passionate longings. The word *philia* means love based on the affection friends show one another.

The word *storge* describes love between family members. Lastly but important is the greatest love for Christians—*agape* love. This is a pure and unselfish love that flows from the goodness of the giver to the needs of the receiver.

Oftentimes we use the Greek word *agape* along with the word *love* (as used in the last paragraph) when we speak of God's love. However, even the word *agape* just doesn't seem appropriate at times because God's love toward us is so boundless and incomprehensible that there seems to be no adequate word to describe it.

In John 15:13 Jesus says, "Greater love hath no man than this, that a man lay down his life for his friends" (KJV). God loved us so much that He sent His one and only darling Son, Jesus, to earth to provide a way for us to escape spiritual death. Likewise, Jesus' love for us resulted in His voluntarily giving the supreme sacrifice of His own life so whosoever believed in Him should be saved. That's love!

Anyone who wants to live a life of love must have God in him to demonstrate the characteristics of love described in 1 Corinthians 13:4–8, which states:

> "Love is patient, love is kind. It does not envy, it does not boast, it is not proud. It does not dishonor others, it is not self-seeking, it is not easily angered, it keeps no record of wrongs. Love does not delight in evil but rejoices with the truth.

It always protects, always trusts, always hopes, always perseveres. Love never fails" (NIV).

A Christian overcomes the world's temptations.

> For whatever is born of God overcomes the world. And this is the victory that has overcome the world—our faith. Who is he who overcomes the world, but he who believes that Jesus is the Son of God? (1 John 5:4–5 NKJV)

In the second and third chapters of Revelation, Jesus describes the rewards for overcomers.

1. For the one who has worked hard, has persevered, has endured hardships for Jesus' name, and has not forsaken his love for one another and/or for Christ, the overcomer will enjoy life forever with Jesus. (See Revelation 2:2-3, 4, 7.)
2. To him who suffers for Christ and is faithful to Him, the overcomer will receive eternal life with Jesus and will not be cast into the lake of fire - hell. (See Revelation 2:10–11.)
3. For the one who remains faithful in the midst of sinfulness and repents of his sins, the overcomer will

receive life here and in eternity and a new name in heaven. (See Revelation 2:13, 16–17.)

4. For the one who gives love, faithful service, perseveres, and do not holds to the teachings of evil ones, the overcomer will receive power and royalty—Jesus Himself. (See Revelation 2:19, 24, 26–28.)

5. To the one who obeys God's Word, repents, and has been redeemed, the overcomer will walk with Jesus. Also, Jesus will not blot his name out of the Book of Life and will acknowledge his name before God and His angels. (See Revelation 3:3, 5.)

6. For the overcomer who has little strength yet keeps God's Word, does not deny His name, and endures patiently, Jesus will make him a permanent pillar in heaven. Jesus will also write the city of God's name, "New Jerusalem," and Jesus' new name upon him. (See Revelation 3:8, 10, 12.)

7. For he who accepts Christ's love and discipline, and loves Him more than worldly possessions, Jesus will grant the overcomer permission to sit with Him on His throne. (See Revelation 3:17–19, 21.)

In addition to the sixteen Christian characteristics, presented above, Galatians 5:19–23 provides a list of the acts of the sinful nature and a list of the fruit of the Spirit. The fruit of the Spirit are the principles and habits produced by the Holy Spirit.

Acts of the Sinful Nature	Fruit of the Spirit
Adultery*	Love
Fornication*	Joy
Uncleanness (Impurity)	Peace
Lasciviousness (Exciting sexual desires)	Long Suffering (Patience)
Idolatry**	Gentleness (Kindness)
Witchcraft	Goodness
Hatred	Faith (Faithfulness)
Variance (Discord)	Meekness (Gentleness)
Emulations (Jealousy)	Temperance (Self-control)
Wrath (Fits of Rage) Resentful anger	
Strife (Violent dissensions) Bitter conflict	
Seditions (Factions) Rebellion	
Heresies (Faction) Chosen Opinion	
Envy	
Murder	
Drunkenness	
Reveling (Uproarious festivities)	

*These sexual sins are usually considered as voluntary sexual intercourse between a man and a woman who are not married to one another. However, Jesus said that anyone who looks at a woman in a lustful manner has already committed adultery with her in his heart. (See Matthew 5:28.)

**Just about anyone or anything can become an idol if the person's love for it is greater than his love for God.

The acts of the sinful nature and the fruit of the Spirit, as shown above, are not all-inclusive lists of bad and good deeds for a Christian. There are many other sins Christians can commit than those listed above. Likewise, there are many other good principles and habits Christians can have than those listed as the fruit of the Spirit. God looks at a person's heart, including his motives, to determine if actions are good or bad. (See 1 Samuel 16:7.) Although Christians may do good deeds to help people, their actions are in vain if they are not motivated by the love of Christ.

One way for Christians to control or conquer the acts of the sinful nature is to become totally dependent on the Lord. This is one of the hardest things for some Christians to learn. To become dependent on the Lord, Christians must have worldly thoughts, attitudes, and allegiances pruned from them.

This pruning process can be compared to the care of fruit-bearing plants. To improve the size of the fruit, farmers and fruit growers must remove the suckers, which are parts of the plant that draw life from it but may not yield fruit. By removing the suckers, the nourishment that would go to the suckers can go to the fruit on the plant, thereby making the fruit larger. The plant also looks better because it does not have all those suckers overcrowding it. The removal of the suckers or shoots is called pruning.

A good example of God's pruning can be seen in the life of King David. At one point, God was displeased with David because he committed adultery with a woman named Bathsheba and caused her to become pregnant. In an attempt to hide his sin, David plotted to have Uriah, Bathsheba's husband, murdered. Knowing King David's heart, God used Nathan, a prophet, to initiate His pruning. Nathan presented a most striking and unique parable to David to point out the severity of David's sinful actions. (See 2 Samuel 12.) Through this parable, God helped David to see an area in his life that required pruning. David knew God's love and power. Therefore he willingly acknowledged his sins. He exclaimed, "I have sinned against the Lord" (2 Samuel 12:13 KJV). This event was a major turning point in David's spiritual life.

Sometimes God's pruning causes Christians to undergo sufferings. When these difficulties arise, we should remember to rejoice because God knows what is best for His children. The apostle Paul said that we should "glory in our sufferings, because we know that suffering produces perseverance; perseverance, character; and character, hope. And hope does not put us to shame, because God's love has been poured out into our hearts through the Holy Spirit, who has been given to us" (Romans 5:3–5 NIV). When Christians endure hardships for Christ's sake, they grow in their faith and have closer relationships with God.

Christians grow in their faith by obtaining knowledge of God, Jesus, and the Holy Spirit and by applying that knowledge to their lives. To gain spiritual knowledge, Christians must continually study and meditate on God's Word and pray for understanding. Valuable sources for gaining understanding of God's Word are spiritual leaders, such as pastors, evangelists, prophets, and teachers. Therefore Christians must carefully choose their spiritual leaders to ensure that the leaders are true spokesmen for God.

CHAPTER 4

Choosing the One to Follow

During the first year of physical life, a child can be trained to recognize one person as his father. So it is with spiritual life. Training is a little more difficult because the spiritual newborn cannot physically see his Father. Satan continually puts many gods before the spiritual newborn and all Christians. Joshua, the successor of Moses, challenged the children of Israel to put away other gods and to serve the Lord. Joshua 24:14–15 says,

> Now therefore fear the Lord, and serve him in sincerity and in truth: and put away the gods which your fathers served on the other side of the flood, and in Egypt; and serve ye the Lord. And if it seem evil unto you to serve the Lord, choose you this day whom ye will serve; whether the gods

which your fathers served that were on the other side of the flood, or the gods of the Amorites, in whose land ye dwell: but as for me and my house, we will serve the LORD. (KJV)

When a child has a good relationship with his father, the child runs to him in times of trouble, when he needs love, comfort, or a friend, or when he is afraid or hungry. Likewise, Christians can find these same securities and many more when they go to God, their heavenly Father.

Just as relationships between children and parents are important, a Christian's relationship to God is important. In the Ten Commandments, God reveals that He is a jealous God and does not want His people to put other gods before Him. (See Exodus 20:3–17.) The first four commandments are about the Christian's relationship with God. The remaining six are about the Christian's relationships with others. Christians should have a better relationship with God, the Father, than they have with anyone or anything else.

Jesus emphasized the importance of putting God first when He responded to the question from a Jewish religious leader, a Pharisee, who was testing Him. (See Matthew 22:35–40.) The Pharisee inquired, "Master, which is the great commandment in the law?" (Matthew 22:36 KJV). Jesus replied in verses 37–39, "Thou shalt love the Lord thy God with all thy heart, and with all thy soul, and with all thy mind. This is the first and great commandment. And the second is like unto it, Thou shalt love thy neighbor as thyself" (KJV).

In addition to people, there are many things Satan may tempt Christians to put first in their lives. When Christians put people or things before God, they are worshipping them. Therefore, Christians must not love money, televisions, automobiles, people, themselves, sports, clothing, accomplishments, buildings, or anyone or anything more than they love God.

Sometimes it is difficult to identify or admit to the things we give first priority in our lives. One way to determine if something is a god, or is on its way to becoming a god, is to honestly consider how you use your time, money, and talents (abilities). In general, Christians give the greatest amount of time, money, and abilities to what they love the most.

When examining what you do with your time, ask yourself the following questions:

1. Am I giving at least 10 percent (average 2.4 hours per day) to God by reading and studying the Bible, testifying, or helping others? If not, look at each activity that takes up the most time and determine whether or not you can eliminate or reduce your involvement. (However, allow for quality time with your family.)

2. How many hours do I usually spend watching television? Could some of that time be spent helping someone in need?

When examining how you use your money, ask yourself:

1. Am I giving at least 10 percent to God's work? If not, determine where your money is going by examining your checkbook(s), credit card accounts, and other similar financial accounting.
2. Is a large amount of my money spent on a particular item, such as a house or automobile? If so, find ways to reduce those expenses so you can give at least ten percent to God's work.

When considering the use of God-given abilities (talents), ask yourself:

1. Do I volunteer to help at my place of worship or to help someone in need?
2. Who benefits from my knowledge, skills, and wisdom?
3. Am I using these abilities the way God intended for them to be used or am I using them only for my own financial gain? For example, if you are a singer, do you sing songs that praise God or do you sing songs that

displease Him but primarily bring financial benefits to you?

Even if you are giving 10 percent of your income and time to God's work, periodically evaluate your motives. Why do you give your money, time, and talents to God and to help others? Are you motivated by love or is it to receive personal benefits, such as recognition, tax deductions, or compensation? This self-audit will help you determine if your giving is in vain.

Jesus wants us to be willing to forsake all to follow Him. One example of this is found in Mark 10. A rich young man runs up to Jesus, kneels before Him, and asks what he must do to inherit eternal life. The young man explains that he has kept the following commandments since he was a boy: "You shall not murder, you shall not commit adultery, you shall not steal, you shall not give false testimony, you shall not defraud, honor your father and mother" (Mark 10:18–22 NIV). But Jesus, knowing the man's heart, lovingly asks him to go and sell everything he has and to give it to the poor. The man's face falls, and he sadly leaves because he has great wealth. He also may have sadly left because Jesus' responses made him realize that he did not put God first in his life.

To follow Jesus, you must know who Jesus is and what He wants you to do. Therefore, carefully choose your church, spiritual leaders, and mature Christians to help you learn the Word of God. After all, the Word of God is the road map for your race through this earthly life.

The choosing of a spiritual leader is crucial. As an example, suppose you were physically blind and had to walk through a dangerous, unfamiliar area. If there were several people near you and each one was giving you different directions or instructions, which person would you listen to? Would it make a difference if there were only two people giving you different directions? Would it make a difference if one of the people had given you accurate instructions in the past, you recognized his voice, and knew that person had your best interests at heart? If that person was giving you instructions while the others were too, who would you listen to? As discussed in Chapter 3 of this book, the apostle John warned us not to believe every spirit because many false prophets have gone out into the world. He told us how to recognize the Spirit of our Father in 1 John 4:2–3,

> This is how you can recognize the Spirit of God:
> Every spirit that acknowledges that Jesus Christ
> has come in the flesh is from God, but every spirit
> that does not acknowledge Jesus is not from God.
> This is the spirit of the antichrist, which you have
> heard is coming and even now is already in the
> world. (NIV)

We have a tendency to imitate people we consider to be strong in their faith. Although God uses people to deliver His Word, it's important for Christians, especially new Christians, to imitate Jesus rather than man. Always look to Jesus for knowledge, wisdom, guidance, and all of your needs.

Yes, Jesus was perfect when He lived on earth. Yes, we can never reach His level of perfection. But His life, as described in the Bible, should be our goal. We can aim for the perfection (completeness or maturity) that Jesus described in Matthew 5:48, "Be ye therefore perfect, even as your Father which is in heaven is perfect" (KJV). (Also see 2 Corinthians 13:11.)

Unlike people, who make mistakes and disappoint us because of their human frailties, Jesus will never disappoint us, although sometimes when we are frustrated it may look as if He has disappointed us. However, we must remember God's words in Hebrews 13:5, "... I will never leave thee, nor forsake thee" (KJV).

Just as it is vital to know who we should follow, it is also vital to know who we should not follow. In Matthew, Jesus warned the crowds and His disciples about teachers of the law and the Pharisees. He said,

> The scribes and the Pharisees sit in Moses' seat.
> Therefore whatever they tell you to observe,
> that observe and do, but do not do according to

their works; for they say, and do not do. For they bind heavy burdens, hard to bear, and lay them on men's shoulders; but they themselves will not move them with one of their fingers. But all their works they do to be seen by men. They make their phylacteries broad and enlarge the borders of their garments. They love the best places at feasts, the best seats in the synagogues, greetings in the marketplaces, and to be called by men, 'Rabbi, Rabbi.' (Matt. 23:2–7 NKJV)

We can use His warnings as an excellent guideline to determine who we should not follow.

In addition to the general warning about the teachers of the law and the Pharisees, Jesus presented eight woes in Matthew 23 (NKJV), which we should consider as warnings. (Please note that the New International Version presents only seven woes.) Christians should use these warnings to identify "wolves in sheep's clothing," who are the leaders they should not follow.

Matthew Henry's Commentary on the Whole Bible[1] gives a more detailed explanation of the verses used in these woes.

1. But woe to you, scribes and Pharisees, hypocrites! For you shut up the kingdom of heaven against men; for you

neither go in yourselves, nor do you allow those who are entering to go in. (v. 13)

A hypocrite is a person who acts like someone he is not and may never be. It has been said that a hypocritical Christian is a person who is not himself on Sundays. This woe is for the enemies of the gospel of Christ. Instead of contributing to the salvation of the souls of men, they do all they can to keep people from believing in Christ—thereby preventing them from entering the kingdom of Heaven. Christian leaders should strive to reveal the mysteries of the gospel so their hearers can be guided toward Jesus and His kingdom in a true and proper sense. Hypocritical leaders don't want others to advance beyond them in religion or to become better than they are in other areas. Followers of these leaders will probably reject the gospel because their leader did.

Christian leaders can become like the Pharisees when they adhere to the Scriptures but do not reveal the mysteries of the Bible. They should be careful not to repeat Bible verses that they know—or should know—will only produce short-term joy to their followers. Words that bring only temporary joy will not sustain Christians. However, words that come from study and meditation of God's Word, under the guidance of the Holy Spirit, will come forth in a powerful and wonderful manner, which will convict the hearts of hearers and help them see the beauty of God. This method will produce long-term joy. The goal of Christian leaders should be to help their hearers understand God's Word, see the mysteries of the Bible, and see the sins in their lives.

2. Woe to you, scribes and Pharisees, hypocrites! For you devour widows' houses, and for a pretense make long prayers. Therefore you will receive greater condemnation. (v. 14)

How could someone devour a widow's house? Consider that many widows are in the weakest periods of their lives. They not only have additional responsibilities due to the absence of their husbands, but they miss the men whom they loved and trusted. This makes widows lonely and vulnerable. If there is anyone they should be able to trust, it should be their Christian leaders. However, some crafty, pretentious leaders prey on widows. They may pray long, pretentious prayers to influence widows to give overwhelmingly to their causes. These leaders may continue until they have beguiled the widows into giving everything, even their houses.

God wants gifts we give to the Church to be given out of our love for Him, not man. He commands Christians to care for widows and orphans. Those who take advantage of them will receive greater damnation.

3. Woe to you, scribes and Pharisees, hypocrites! For you travel land and sea to win one proselyte, and when he is won, you make him twice as much a son of hell as yourselves. (v. 15).

Religious leaders are hypocrites when they use all kinds of schemes to "bring souls to Christ." The motives of these hypocritical leaders are not for the glory of God or for the good of the souls, but for their credit.

The converts of hypocritical leaders can become even worse than their leaders. Although these converts claim to be Christians, they are considered sons of hell, because they have become like their father, the devil, the father of lies. Enemies of hypocritical leaders and their converts are people who practice true Christianity.

Although many Christian leaders are sincere, devout, and religious, some become leaders for selfish reasons. Other leaders begin with good motives but later go astray. When this happens, they may develop wrong motives for winning souls for Christ.

A selfish leader may measure the effectiveness of his ministry by the number of people "*he*" brings to Christ. He credits himself for the harvest and glorifies himself, rather than God. When this occurs, more emphasis is usually put on the birth of the new Christian and less emphasis on helping new Christians develop a solid spiritual foundation during their formative years. If new Christians do not receive proper Bible-based teachings, Satan can deceive them into performing the hypocritical acts Jesus referred to in this woe.

4.   Woe to you, blind guides, who say, 'Whoever swears by the temple, it is nothing; but whoever swears by the gold of the temple, he is obliged to perform it.' Fools and blind! For which is greater, the gold or the temple that sanctifies the gold? And, 'Whoever swears by the altar, it is nothing; but whoever swears by the gift that is on it, he is obliged to perform it.' Fools and blind! For which is greater, the gift or the altar that sanctifies the gift? Therefore he who swears by the altar, swears by it and by all things on it. He who swears by the temple, swears by it and by Him who dwells in it. And he who swears by heaven, swears by the throne of God and by Him who sits on it. (vv. 16–22)

The phrase "blind guides" reminds me of the question Jesus asked in His parable in Luke 6:39: "Can the blind lead the blind? Will they not both fall into the ditch?" If the guide is lost how can he lead someone else correctly? The warning is to blind guides, the ones who will be accountable to God. These leaders put more emphasis on the gold of the temple and gifts on the altar than the temple and altar themselves. Their motive is to receive some of the gold and gifts. When they reach this point, they are serving the created—gold and gifts—more than the Creator, God. Jesus informed the blind guides that the holiness of the temple and altar is what makes the gold and gifts sacred. Therefore, the temple and altar can be no less holy than that which is brought to them.

Blind guides consider things sinful or holy based on how it serves their purposes, rather than how it will bring glory to God and enrich the souls of Christians. For example, some religious leaders encourage their followers to bring gifts to the altar; however, their primary purpose is for personal benefit. The gifts and oaths of Christian leaders and followers should be for those purposes, or things, that result in praises and honor to God.

We can pattern our attitude for giving gifts to God by the advice the apostle Paul gave Timothy, his "true son in the faith" (see 1 Timothy 6). This chapter has a phrase that some people misquote—"For the love of money is the root of all evil: ..." (v. 10, KJV). Note that it says the *love* of money is the root of all evil, not the money itself, as implied in the misquote. The apostle Paul's discussion on giving and receiving in 1 Timothy 6:3–12 is so beautiful that it needs repeating here:

> If any man teach otherwise [false doctrine], and
> consent not to wholesome words, even the words
> of our Lord Jesus Christ, and to the doctrine which

is according to godliness; He is proud, knowing nothing, but doting about questions and strifes of words, whereof cometh envy, strife, railings [malicious talk], evil surmisings [suspicions], perverse disputings [constant friction] of men of corrupt minds, and destitute [altogether lacking] of the truth, supposing that gain is godliness: from such withdraw thyself. But godliness with contentment is great gain. For we brought nothing into this world, and it is certain we can carry nothing out. And having food and raiment let us be therewith content. But they that will be rich fall into temptation and a snare, and into many foolish and hurtful lusts, which drown men in destruction and perdition. For the love of money is the root of all evil: which while some coveted after, they have erred from the faith, and pierced themselves through with many sorrows. But thou, O man of God, flee these things; and follow after righteousness, godliness, faith, love, patience, meekness. Fight the good fight of faith, lay hold on eternal life, whereunto thou art also called, and hast professed a good profession before many witnesses.

5. Woe to you, scribes and Pharisees, hypocrites! For you pay tithe of mint and anise and cummin, and have

neglected the weightier matters of the law: justice and mercy and faith. These you ought to have done, without leaving the others undone. Blind guides, who strain out a gnat and swallow a camel. (vv. 23–24).

Hypocritical leaders deceive themselves and mock God by following strict procedures for giving their tithes but neglect more important matters like justice, mercy, and faith. Micah 6:8 (NKJV) states "He has shown you, O man, what *is* good; And what does the Lord require of you But to do justly, To love mercy, and to walk humbly with your God?"

An example of a hypocritical leader is someone who does things primarily for churches or church members who can pay him, or return favors for his services. Therefore, hypocritical leaders "strain out a gnat" by pointing out someone else's "sins," like washing a car on Sunday but neglect to see their sins, like deceivingly taking a widow's house, which would be comparable to swallowing a camel.

As the Scriptures in Matthew and Micah indicate, our relationship with God and our motives and attitudes for doing things for Him are more important than the acts we perform for Him. Christians should not neglect justice, mercy, and humility.

For a practical illustration of these words, let's consider the plight of a motorist who is stopped by a policeman for speeding. Suppose the policeman stops the person for driving sixty miles per hour in a forty-five-mile-per-hour speed zone. Let's suppose the law states the penalty for speeding can be a ticket, a fine, or demerit points added to the driver's driving record.

The policeman would show *injustice* if he opens the car door, snatches the driver from the car, beats him up, and then gives him a ticket for speeding. The driver would receive a penalty more than he deserves and the law requires.

The policeman would show *justice* if he politely explains why he required the driver to stop the car, discusses the penalties for speeding, gives the driver a ticket, and explains options the driver can take. The driver would receive what he deserves.

The policeman would show *mercy* if he politely explains the circumstances for asking the driver to stop his car, discusses the penalties for speeding, and allows the driver to proceed without giving him a ticket. This would be giving the driver what he does not deserve.

The policeman would show *grace* by writing a ticket for the driver, to show he was guilty. But, instead of giving the driver the ticket, the policeman tells the driver he is free to go. The officer submits the ticket to law officials and appears before the judge to accept the driver's punishment. The driver would receive unmerited favor, more than what he deserves.

To walk humbly with your God is not to consider yourself more highly than you ought to. Consider the policeman and speeding driver scenario illustrated above. The policeman could arrogantly consider himself to have authority not only to enforce the law but also to be the law. In his eyes, whatever he says or does would be all right; he could do whatever he wants because he is the law. In this case he would be considering himself more highly than he ought.

However, it is possible for the policeman to have the same confidence in his position of authority but express it in a humble manner. Like the policeman, Christians are in delegated positions of authority where they should humbly walk before God and others. A Christian who wants to walk humbly can ask himself this question before making decisions, "What would Jesus do, or say, in a situation like this?"

6. Woe to you, scribes and Pharisees, hypocrites! For you cleanse the outside of the cup and dish, but inside they are full of extortion and self-indulgence. Blind Pharisee, first cleanse the inside of the cup and dish, that the outside of them may be clean also. (vv. 25–26)

Jesus is referring to leaders who take extra care to look good to others but who are slack in their concern for the way they appear to God. They fail to resolve their problems, such as greed and self-indulgence, on the inside. It's as if they have forgotten that what they are on the inside dictates what they are on the outside.

There are two sayings that are probably based on Jesus' solution in this woe—"First clean the inside of the cup and dish, and then the outside also will be clean." These sayings are: "Actions speak louder than words" and "Your actions speak so loud I can't hear what you are saying." These sayings are reminders that our actions usually reflect what we are on the inside.

Jesus also reminded us of the importance of a clean heart in the Sermon on the Mount. (See Matthew 5:21, 27, 33, 38, 43) Several times He said, "You have heard that it was said…, but I tell you …" Usually the statement after the word "but" referred to a matter of the heart, the center of a person's thinking. He identified the heart as the source that affects the person's true actions.

7. Woe to you, scribes and Pharisees, hypocrites! For you are like whitewashed tombs which indeed appear beautiful outwardly, but inside are full of dead men's bones and all uncleanness. Even so you also outwardly appear righteous to men, but inside you are full of hypocrisy and lawlessness. (vv. 27–28)

In these verses Jesus cautions religious leaders who do things for show. Some people are very good at making themselves look righteous on the outside but have a heart full of sin. What good will their "show" be when they stand before God? Which should we strive for—to hear our friends say "well done," or to hear our Master say "well done, thou good and faithful servant"? (See Matthew 25:14–30)

8. Woe to you, scribes and Pharisees, hypocrites! Because you build the tombs of the prophets and adorn the monuments of the righteous, and say, 'If we had lived in the days of our fathers, we would not have been partakers with them in the blood of the prophets.' Therefore you are witnesses against yourselves that you are sons of those who murdered the prophets. Fill up, then, the measure of your fathers' guilt. (vv. 29–32)

In this warning, Jesus was denouncing the act of pretending to honor the prophets. God wants us to honor and respect His prophets and leaders when they are obedient to Him. However, we are not to put them above Him.

It is easy to say what we could or would have done had we lived in the days of our forefathers. It is also easy to say what we would have done if we had opportunities others had or if we had been confronted with certain temptations. It is easy to say how we would have followed Jesus had we lived during the time He lived on earth. Is He not living with us today? Do we ever see His works in the lives of others? If you had been Peter, one of Jesus' disciples, would you have publicly admitted that you were one of His followers, knowing that you too might have received bodily harm? The last sentence of this woe implies that children cannot always use their forefather's sins as excuses for their sins. Children "fill up the measure of their forefather's sins" when they continue to practice the wrongs of their ancestors.

Christians need to fully understand Jesus' warnings to hypocritical leaders, as discussed above. In doing so, we can gain a better understanding of the characteristics we should look for in our spiritual leaders. Spiritual leaders will also gain a better understanding of the characteristics they should personally attain. Christians are to follow Jesus and His consecrated spiritual leaders among us.

When choosing who to follow, we must also keep in mind Proverbs 3:5–6, which tell us to "Trust in the LORD with all thine heart; and lean not unto thine own understanding. In all thy ways acknowledge him, and he shall direct thy paths" (KJV). Knowing who we should follow and trusting the Lord are crucial steps for us as Christians if we want to put our faith into action, thereby practicing Christianity.

CHAPTER 5

Practicing Christianity

Becoming born again (saved) is just the beginning of our spiritual race or journey. As Christians learn about God, they must also learn how to apply that knowledge and wisdom to their daily lives. Their motivation to practice Christianity is based on their love for Jesus Christ, their Lord and Savior. This chapter provides information that will encourage us to practice Christianity by putting our faith into action. James, the brother of Jesus, says, "But be ye doers of the word, and not hearers only, deceiving your own selves" (James 1:22 KJV). Putting your faith into action requires studying and hearing God's Word, reading Christian literature, and receiving revelations from the Holy Spirit.

God's Word provides instructions to help us practice Christianity. Consider the apostle Paul's words in 1

Thessalonians 5:12–22 (NIV). His instructions, in a list format, are:

- "Acknowledge those who work hard among you, who care for you in the Lord and who admonish you. Hold them in the highest regard in love because of their work" (v. 12).
- "Live in peace with each other" (v. 13).
- "Warn those who are idle and disruptive" (v. 14).
- "Encourage the disheartened" (v. 14).
- "Help the weak" (v. 14).
- "Be patient with everyone" (v. 14).
- "Make sure that nobody pays back wrong for wrong, but always strive to do what is good for each other and for everyone else" (v. 15).
- "Rejoice always" (v. 16).
- "Pray continually" (v. 17).
- "Give thanks in all circumstances; for this is God's will for you in Christ Jesus" (v. 18).
- "Do not quench the Spirit" (v. 19).
- "Do not treat prophecies with contempt but test them all" (vv. 19-21).
- "Hold on to what is good" (v. 21).
- "Reject every kind of evil" (v. 22).

To follow these instructions, Christians must understand a basic requirement for practicing Christianity as found in Romans 12:2. It states, "Do not conform to the pattern of this world, but be transformed by the renewing of your mind. Then you will be able to test and approve what God's will is—his good, pleasing and perfect will" (NIV). The key part of this verse is, "but be transformed by the renewing of your mind."

The apostle Paul advises us in Ephesians 4:17 that we must no longer live a life without God. In verses 22–24, he also says, "You were taught, with regard to your former way of life, to put off your old self, which is being corrupted by its deceitful desires; to be made new in the attitude of your minds; and to put on the new self, created to be like God in true righteousness and holiness" (NIV). In Romans 4:17–5:21, Paul gives us examples of the former way of life and the new life.

Paul's teachings show us that practicing Christianity involves a process of changing the mind. Transforming your mind from the old way of thinking to a new way of thinking involves three key steps:

1. Examining yourself (self-examination)
2. Developing right attitudes
3. Praising God

1. Self-Examination

Examining yourself in the light of God's Word reveals those areas where you need to change or to renew your mind. After King David examined his sins involving Bathsheba, he wrote Psalm 51. He said in verse 10 of this psalm, "Create in me a clean heart, O God; and renew a right spirit within me" (KJV).

As part of your self-examination, consider these crucial areas: anger, self-pride, influences, sources of happiness, and religious teachings.

A. Anger

Your ability to control anger is important in all relationships. The apostle Paul tells us in Ephesians 4:26, "Be ye angry, and sin not: let not the sun go down upon your wrath" (KJV). Does this verse tell us not to get angry? No! It tells us to deal with our anger. We should resolve our anger as soon as possible. If we don't, it could cause us to do something wrong, which then may be sinful. James 1:19–20 warns us, "Let every man be swift to hear, slow to speak, slow to wrath; for the wrath of man does not produce the righteousness of God" (NKJV).

When you become angry with someone, evaluate the circumstances. Determine if you are angry with the person or the person's actions. By focusing on the actions, you may realize that the source of the problem is you or Satan rather than the other person. Then you can get angry with yourself or Satan. Paul said in Ephesians 6:12, "For our struggle is not against flesh and blood, but against the rulers, against the authorities, against the powers of this dark world and against the spiritual forces of evil in the heavenly realms" (NIV).

If you believe the other person is the source of the problem, try resolving your differences by applying the guidance in Matthew 18:15-17.

> If your brother sins against you, go and tell him his fault between you and him alone. If he hears you, you have gained your brother. But if he will not hear, take with you one or two more, that 'by the mouth of two or three witnesses every word may be established.' And if he refuses to hear them, tell it to the church. But if he refuses even to hear the church, let him be to you like a heathen and a tax collector. (NKJV)

When Jesus got angry, He controlled His righteous anger so that He would not sin. Mark 3:1-6 reveals how Jesus responded to anger. The Pharisees watched Jesus closely to see if He would heal on the Sabbath, which they considered sinful. They were looking for a reason to accuse Him. The fifth verse states, "He [Jesus] looked around at them in anger and, deeply distressed at their stubborn hearts, said to the man, 'Stretch out your hand'" (NIV). Note that Jesus was angry at the Pharisees' stubborn hearts and not at the men themselves. He was in control of His anger, and His anger did not control Him.

B. Self-Pride

Another culprit to look for is self-pride, which refers to your feelings about yourself. Self-pride is important. Having a sense of self-worth as well as a desire to be somebody who achieves goals is healthy. However, if it leads to self-exaltation, conceit, or feelings of superiority, it becomes harmful. Desires become harmful when they become unbalanced, lustful, and cause you to crave things that are forbidden or exceed your ability to control them. For example, harmful desires develop when a person has been taught or has gained the wrong attitude toward a person or thing. Abuse can occur when a person has the wrong attitude toward another person.

C. Influences

Examine the actions of the people with whom you associate to determine who influences you. If you are regularly around people who talk about others, tell jokes that degrade God and others, or encourage you to do sinful things, you will have a hard time practicing Christianity. Therefore, you must remove yourself from those influences, even if you have to move to another area or change friends. However, remember you are removing yourself because you realize your weakness and not because you feel superior to your old friends. As Christians, our contact with unsaved people should be to influence them to accept Christ and not to be influenced by them so compromise our beliefs. All Christians need positive encouragement, which is more likely to come from fellow Christians.

D. Sources of Happiness

Another area to examine is what makes you joyful or truly happy. The writer of the book of Ecclesiastes, the "teacher" as he called himself, investigated this question, "What profit hath a man of all his labour which he taketh under the sun?" (Ecclesiastes 1:3 KJV). He wanted to understand what brought true happiness. He gave his heart to seek and search for wisdom until he said "Lo, I am come to great estate, and have gotten more wisdom than all they that have been before me in Jerusalem: yea, my heart had great experience of wisdom and knowledge" (Ecclesiastes 1:16 KJV). However, he states in the eighteenth verse, "For in much wisdom is much grief: and he that increaseth knowledge increaseth sorrow" (KJV).

The writer explained, in detail, how he tried drinking, built beautiful houses and gardens, had slaves, had many wives and women, acquired much silver and gold, and did everything he thought would be worthwhile for men to do. After trying all of these things, he said they were "vanity" (meaningless). However, his efforts were not in vain because he discovered what was truly meaningful. His conclusion is stated in the last two verses of the book, "Let us hear the conclusion of the whole matter: Fear God, and keep his commandments: for this is the whole duty of man. For God shall bring every work into judgment, with every secret thing, whether it be good, or whether it be evil" (Ecclesiastes 12:13–14 KJV).

If we include God in everything we do, the outcome will be joyous and will make life meaningful.

E. Religious teachings

Sometimes renewing the mind requires Christians to change some religious teachings they have previously believed. For example, there was a time when I had to examine my earlier beliefs when someone said he was going to heaven when he died. My question was, how could someone know the decision God would make at the judgment? In Matthew

25:31-46, Jesus said that at the judgment he would separate the saved from the unsaved as a shepherd would separate the sheep from the goats.

My misunderstanding of the judgment prevented me from saying that I would go to heaven when I died. To my surprise, there were others, including religious leaders, who could not show me the error in my logic or thinking.

Through studying the Bible, listening to Bible teachings, and the Holy Spirit intervening, God showed me my problem. Somehow I had the impression that at the last judgment God would determine who would go to heaven or to hell. One piece of incorrect information prevented me from having a better understanding of this portion of the Bible. What a revelation I gained when I read and understood Revelation 20:11-15, which reveals that the judgment is for rewards and not for determining who will be saved. The apostle John says in Revelation 20:12-13, and 15,

> And I saw the dead, small and great, stand before God; and the books were opened: and another book was opened, which is the book of life: and the dead were judged out of those things which were written in the books, *according to their works.* And the sea gave up the dead which were in it; and death and hell delivered up the dead which were in them: and they were judged every man

according to their works. And whosoever was not found written in the book of life was cast into the lake of fire. (KJV, emphasis mine)

It is by God's grace and not by our works that we are saved. (See Ephesians 2:8–9.) At the judgment seat of Christ, the saved (those whose names are written in the Book of Life) will receive their rewards for the works they did for God while on the earth. (See 2 Corinthians 5:10.) Likewise the unsaved will be judged by their works but at a different judgment, which is described in Revelation 20. Therefore the decisions we make to accept or reject Christ as our personal Savior and Lord during our days on earth determines whether we will spend eternity in heaven or in the lake of fire.

Once we make the decision to accept Jesus Christ as our Lord and Savior and become committed to following Him, we have eternal security. Jesus says in John 10:27–29, "My sheep listen to my voice; I know them, and they follow me. I give them eternal life, and they shall never perish; no one will snatch them out of my hand. My Father, who has given them to me, is greater than all; no one can snatch them out of my Father's hand" (NIV).

2. Developing Right Attitudes

In Philippians 2:5, the apostle Paul said that our attitude should be the same as that of Christ Jesus. To change our attitudes to that of Jesus Christ, we must renew our attitudes. For example, some Christians have trouble showing humility or meekness. Some believe meekness shows the weakness of a person. But humility and meekness involve our attitudes toward other people. These characteristics require Christians to control their mental and physical power. They also require that Christians not think of themselves more highly than they ought to. (See Romans 12:3.)

There are several common areas where a Christian can develop right attitudes: prayer, temptation, favoritism, good and evil, and giving.

A. Prayer

One of the most important right attitudes for Christians to develop is the correct attitude towards prayer. Basically, prayer is communication with God, which is a powerful tool for Christians. The apostle Paul told the Thessalonians that we are to pray continually. Although God has an abundance of all things, our prayers should consist of more than requests for physical things. Through prayer, we can thank and praise God for what He has done for us, ask Him for guidance and forgiveness, intercede on behalf of others, and seek God's will for our lives. We should humbly approach God and expect one of four answers: "Yes," "Wait," "No," or "I (God) have something better for you." All four answers require Christians to be patient, to trust and have faith in God, and to love God. However, the answers "No," "Wait," and, "I have something better for you," seem to present the greatest challenges to Christians.

There are many instances when God answers requests immediately. For example, 2 Kings 6:17 states, "And Elisha prayed, and said, LORD, I pray thee, open his eyes, that he may see. And the LORD opened the eyes of the young man; and he saw: and, behold, the mountain was full of horses and chariots of fire round about Elisha" (KJV). Acts 16:26 records another example of an immediate response to prayer. It reveals that when Paul and Silas were in prison, they prayed at midnight and sang praises to God and great results occurred: "And suddenly there was a great earthquake, so that the foundations of the prison were shaken: and immediately all the doors were opened, and every one's bands were loosed" (KJV).

When God's answer is yes, it may be manifested immediately or later, which is why Christians must learn to trust God and wait on Him. Consider God's answer to the prayer of Zechariah and Elizabeth, the parents of John the Baptist. They were probably in their sixties or seventies and did not have children. However, Luke 1:13 states, "But the angel said to him: 'Do not be afraid, Zechariah; your prayer has been heard. Your wife Elizabeth will bear you a son, and you are to call him John'" (NIV). Zachariah's response was, "How can I be sure of this? I am an old man and my wife is well along in years" (Luke 1:18 NIV). His response indicates he may have been praying for a child for a long time.

The answer "no" is usually hard to accept, no matter who it comes from. However, when God says "no," it is always for our benefit. In Matthew 26:36–44, Jesus prayed three times for "this cup" to pass from Him. He was asking God to remove or shorten the suffering He was about to go through. However, He finally said "O my Father, if this cup may not pass away from me, except I drink it, thy will be done" (Matthew 26:42 KJV). Even though God did not remove the cup, He did give Jesus strength to endure His sufferings.

When God gives us something that is better for us than we requested, His answer may not be noticeable to us. Therefore, we may think He did not respond to our request. However, when we don't get what we requested, we should look for another possible answer to our request other than the one we expected.

B. Temptation

Developing the right attitude toward temptations involves knowing the origins of them. James 1:13–14 states, "Let no one say when he is tempted, 'I am tempted by God'; for God cannot be tempted by evil, nor does He Himself tempt anyone. But each one is tempted when he is drawn away by his own desires and enticed" (NKJV). Therefore, on those days when you confront Satan's temptations, remember 1 Corinthians 10:13, which states, "There hath no temptation taken you but such as is common to man: but God is faithful, who will not suffer you to be tempted above that ye are able; but will with the temptation also make a way to escape, that ye may be able to bear it" (KJV).

C. Favoritism

In James 2:1-12, the apostle James instructs us about favoritism toward the rich and poor. He says if we give respect to someone who comes in our assembly wearing nice clothes and not to someone who looks poor, we sin. In the eighth and ninth verses he states, "If ye fulfill the royal law according to the scripture, Thou shalt love thy neighbor as thyself, ye do well: But if ye have respect to persons, ye commit sin, and are convinced of the law as transgressors" (KJV). These verses in James are not telling us to hate the rich and love the poor. Rather, God wants us to love our rich or poor neighbor as we love ourselves. Therefore, when you meet or entertain people, treat each one in the same way no matter how they are dressed or what credentials they may have.

Another reason why we should not show favoritism or discrimination against others can be found in Matthew 25:31–46. In these verses, Jesus reveals a parable about sheep and goats to describe the criteria that He, the King, will use to separate people when they stand before Him on judgment day. The King will separate them as a shepherd divides sheep from goats. He will put the sheep, the righteous, on His right and the goats, the unrighteous, on His left.

The King tells the righteous that they will inherit the kingdom prepared for them since the creation of the world and explains to them, "For I was an hungred, and ye gave me meat: I was thirsty, and ye gave me drink: I was a stranger, and ye took me in: Naked, and ye clothed me: I was sick, and ye visited me: I was in prison, and ye came unto me" (Matt. 25:35–36 KJV).

In their reply to the King, the righteous said, "Lord, when did we see you hungry and feed you, or thirsty and give you something to drink? When did we see you a stranger and invite you in, or needing clothes and clothe you? When did we see you sick or in prison and go to visit you?" (Matthew 25:37–39 NIV).

When the King addresses the unrighteous, He tells them to depart from Him into the eternal fire prepared for the devil and his angels. They had not shown compassion for the hungry, thirsty, strangers, sick, or prisoners. Ironically, their reply was similar to the one of the righteous. Since the unrighteous didn't remember doing anything wrong to the King or the ones He named, their reply may have been a question to seek clarification or an excuse.

Interestingly, the King's response to the unrighteous was similar to His response to the righteous. He said to the unrighteous, "Verily I say unto you, Inasmuch as ye did it not to one of the least of these, ye did it not to me" (Matthew 25:40 KJV). To the righteous He said, "Verily I say unto you, Inasmuch as ye have done it unto one of the least of these my brethren, ye have done it unto me" (Matthew 25:45 KJV).

The King, or the Judge, will remember what we do or don't do for the "least of these." Therefore, we must be careful how we treat the poor, the hungry, the thirsty, strangers, ones in need of clothes, the sick, and prisoners. What we do to them, we do likewise to Christ.

D. Good and Evil

A good attitude to have toward good and evil is stated in Amos 5:14–15, which says, "Seek good, not evil, that you may live. Then the LORD God Almighty will be with you, just as you say he is. Hate evil, love good; maintain justice in the courts" (NIV).

In America, attitudes toward the value of human life have gradually changed through the years. Increasingly, teenagers and young adults seem to have less respect for themselves and others. Thousands of babies are also aborted each day. These circumstances did not reach staggering magnitudes overnight. Gradual change is a tactic Satan uses to lure people into sin, to deceive people into changing their attitudes about sin, and to confuse people about what is right and wrong. Therefore, Christians must constantly evaluate their attitudes based on God's instructions as stated in the Bible rather than comparing their attitudes to those of other people, including Christians.

E. Giving

A good attitude to have toward giving is to give without expecting anything in return. This attitude brings joy to the giver and the recipient. Jesus said, "It is more blessed to give than to receive" (Acts 20:35 KJV). However, our giving should not be a thoughtless process. We should strive to be good stewards of what God gives us. Some Christians believe in giving to anyone, even if the person chooses to use the gift for the wrong purpose. Following that belief without guidance from the Holy Spirit may result in us becoming poor stewards of the possessions God gives us.

I have had several personal experiences that have shown me how to respond to people who ask me for money. One year, my church was providing temporary housing for a man who was out of work and didn't have any money. When he told me he didn't have any food, I decided to give him ten dollars. The next day, a friend of mine told me the man had purchased alcohol the same evening I had given him money—most likely with the money I had given him. This lesson taught me to be careful to whom I give money. My money could have caused the man to hurt himself or others.

Later, this experience proved to be a hindrance and a help. One day just as I was exiting a grocery store, a little boy asked me for money, but I didn't give him any. On the way to my car and while loading my groceries, I thought about my reaction to the child. Before leaving, I went back to the store entrance, but the child was gone. Then I wondered if I had missed helping "one of the least of these."

After these two experiences, I was better prepared to respond to a lady who approached me in the parking lot of the same grocery store a few days later. She asked me for fifty cents to help her buy food. I offered to go with her inside the store and buy her food. But she said she could buy food at a lower price somewhere else. Her response caused me to think she wanted money for something other than food. Therefore, I did not give her any money. When I told my wife, she asked a thought-provoking question, "You were giving her the food. How could she get it cheaper somewhere else?"

Everyone should have a good attitude toward giving. Even if you consider yourself to be "one of the least of these," you can still give. Consider the poor widow woman of Zarephath.

And when he [the prophet Elijah] came to the gate of the city, behold, the widow woman was there gathering of sticks: and he called to her, and said, Fetch me, I pray thee a little water in a vessel, that I may drink. And as she was going to fetch it, he called to her, and said, Bring me, I pray thee, a morsel of bread in thine hand. And she said, As the Lord thy God liveth, I have not a cake, but an handful of meal in a barrel, and a little oil in a cruse: and, behold, I am gathering two sticks, that I may go in and dress it for me and my son, that we may eat it, and die. And Elijah said unto her, Fear not; go and do as thou hast said: but make me thereof a little cake first, and bring it unto me, and after make for thee and for thy son." "And she went and did according to the saying of Elijah:

and she, and he, and her house, did eat many days. And the barrel of meal wasted not, neither did the cruse of oil fail, according to the word of the Lord, which he spake by Elijah. (1 Kings 17:10–13, 15–16 KJV)

The prophet Elijah asked the poor widow to give him the first cake from the last handful of her meal. God had a blessing for her if she had the right attitude of giving. Since she obeyed Elijah, her household was able to eat for many days.

3. Praising God

Psalm 150:6 says, "Let every thing that hath breath praise the Lord" (KJV). When we consider how much God has done for us and what He has brought us through, we should give Him honor and praises. We should also tell others about His goodness toward us. Several examples from the Bible can encourage us to have an attitude of thankfulness and praise. We should glorify God, give God credit, tell others about God, praise God, and always rejoice.

A. Glorify God

One day when Jesus was entering a village, ten lepers asked Him to have mercy on them. When Jesus saw them, He told them to go show themselves to the priests. (This was a normal procedure after being cured of leprosy.) On their way to the priests, the lepers were healed. However, only one of the ten lepers returned to glorify God. He fell down on his face at Jesus' feet and thanked Him. In Luke 17:17–19, Jesus asked, "'Were there not ten cleansed? but where are the nine?' And he said unto him, 'Arise, go thy way: thy faith hath made thee whole'" (KJV).

B. Give God Credit

After Jesus healed a blind man on a Sabbath day, the Pharisees questioned the man and his parents. (See John 9:1–34.) His parents feared the Jews because the Pharisees said that if any man confessed that Jesus was Christ, he would be put out of the synagogue. When the Jews asked them how their son, who was born blind, could now see, they told them to ask their son. The Jews asked the son to give God the praise instead of Jesus. They thought Jesus was a sinner. However, the son answered, "Whether he be a sinner or no, I know not: one thing I know, that, whereas I was blind, now I see" (John 9:25 KJV).

C. Tell Others about God

At Jacob's well in the city of Samaria, Jesus had a heart-to-heart talk with a woman. (See John 4:1-42.) She had come for water, but Jesus offered her "living water." He revealed her immoral lifestyle and acknowledged that He was the Messiah and the Christ. After His disciples returned, the woman went into the city and said to the men, "Come, see a man, which told me all things that ever I did: is not this the Christ?" (John 4:29 KJV). The results of her testimony are stated in verse 39, "And many of the Samaritans of that city believed on him for the saying of the woman, which testified, He told me all that ever I did" (KJV).

D. Praise God

A certain man, who had been lame from his mother's womb, asked the apostles Peter and John for money as they entered the temple. (See Acts 3:1-10.) They looked at the man and Peter said, "Silver and gold have I none; but such as I have give I thee: In the name of Jesus Christ of Nazareth rise up and walk. And he took him by the right hand, and lifted him up: and immediately his feet and ankle bones received strength. And he leaping up stood, and walked, and entered with them into the temple, walking, and leaping, and praising God" (Acts 3:6–8 KJV).

In verses 12–16 of this same chapter, Peter acknowledged Jesus as the source of the healing. He said that it was not his or John's own power or holiness that healed the man. In addition to the lame man praising God, Peter and John also praised Him for the healing.

E. Always Rejoice

The apostle Paul admonished us to "rejoice in the Lord always" (Philippians 4:4 KJV). He was able to rejoice because he had learned how to be content. He said in Philippians 4:11–13:

> "Not that I speak in respect of want: for I have learned, in whatsoever state I am, therewith to be content. I know both how to be abased, and I know how to abound: every where and in all things I am instructed both to be full and to be hungry, both to abound and to suffer need. I can do all things through Christ which strengtheneth me" (KJV).

As you seek ways to practice your Christianity, remember you are responsible for your destiny. You must determine how to put your faith into action. Yes, other Christians can help, but you are responsible for working out your own salvation. (See Philippians 2:12.) You must "study to shew thyself approved unto God, a workman that needeth not to be ashamed, rightly dividing the word of truth" (2 Timothy 2:15 KJV). To accomplish these things, you must take responsibility for renewing your mind and changing your attitudes.

You may ask, "How can I renew my mind? How can I help someone transform his mind? How does a person gain or receive attitudes? How does a person develop good or bad attitudes?" Possible answers and profound truths are revealed in the following poem.

Christians Learn What They Live
(Revised from "Children Learn What They Live")[1]

If a Christian lives with criticism,

    He learns to condemn.

If a Christian lives with hostility,

    He learns to fight.

If a Christian lives with ridicule,

    He learns to be shy.

If a Christian lives with shame,

    He learns to feel guilty.

If a Christian lives with tolerance,

    He learns to be patient.

If a Christian lives with encouragement,

    He learns confidence.

If a Christian lives with praise,

He learns to appreciate.

If a Christian lives with fairness,

He learns justice.

If a Christian lives with security,

He learns to have faith.

If a Christian lives with approval,

He learns to like himself.

If a Christian lives with acceptance and friendship,

He learns to find love in the world.

Replacing the word *child* with the word *Christian* in this poem presents another interesting analogy between a child and a Christian. After all, a born-again person is a child of God who has a new spiritual life.

Remember Jesus' words to Nicodemus, "You must be born again" (John 3:7 NIV). A true spiritual birth is required to become a Christian. However, a new birth is only the beginning of the spiritual race or journey. To win, we must obey God's Word, choose godly leaders to help us develop excellent Christian characteristics, and practice our Christian beliefs and faith.

Finally, we must follow the apostle Paul's instructions to,

Lay aside every weight, and the sin which doth so easily beset us, and let us run with patience the race that is set before us, Looking unto Jesus the author and finisher of our faith; who for the joy that was set before him endured the cross, despising the shame, and is set down at the right hand of the throne of God. (Hebrews 12:1–2 KJV)

Then when the race is completed, we will hear our Lord say, "Well done, thou good and faithful servant: ... enter thou into the joy of thy lord" (Matthew 25:21 KJV).

About the Author

The teaching ministry of Eric Jackson spans more than forty-five years. Inspired by the Scripture, "My people are destroyed for lack of knowledge" (Hosea 4:6 KJV), he has helped people of all ages gain knowledge and understanding of the Word of God.

In 1962, Eric heard a song that would change the course of his life. While attending church with his wife in Atlanta, Georgia, he heard a young blind girl sing a song titled, "If I Can Help Somebody," by A.B. Antrozzo. As the girl sang of the virtue of serving your fellow man, the words were crystallized in Eric's mind. This experience motivated him to dedicate his life to teaching.

As a result of his dedication, he was nicknamed "Old Faithful" by inmates of City Farm, a Newport News, Virginia based correctional facility (a minimum security prison), where he helped lead a weekly Bible study for more than twenty-five years. He also helped teach adult and young adult Sunday school classes.

In addition to teaching, Eric served as president of the Peninsula Trustees Council (1990–1994) and chairman of the Children's Home Committee for a Union of Newport News Sunday schools.

A native of Meherrin, Virginia, Eric is a graduate of Howard University and the University of Virginia and was a licensed mechanical engineer until his retirement. He resides in Newport News with his wife, Celestine. Eric is the father of Eric Jr., who is married to Ellen, and Cheryl, who is married to Virgil Tyler. He is the grandfather of Selena Jackson, Karina Jackson, and Virgil Tyler Jr.

Notes

Chapter 2: Becoming a Christian

1. Reprinted from *High School Teacher Sunday School Book*, Summer 1993 (Cincinnati, Ohio: Standard Publishing Company) Used by permission.

Chapter 4: Choosing the One to Follow

1. For a detailed discussion of the eight woes, see Matthew Henry's Commentary on the Whole Bible.

Chapter 5: Practicing Christianity

1. Author unknown

CPSIA information can be obtained at www.ICGtesting.com
Printed in the USA
BVOW08s1941210216

437268BV00003B/6/P